t's Raining Cats

A Collection of Common English Idioms

and

Colloquialisms

by

Steve Ellis

Dedication

To all my students and local non-native English speaking teachers in Thailand, Malaysia, Italy and Turkey, whom I have enjoyed teaching and training and with whom I have had fun as they explored using English idioms, everyday sayings and phrasal verbs.

··· ··· ··· ··· ··· ··· ··· ··· ··· ···

For friendly, personalised, one -to- one video lessons to help you improve your English
Please visit:

English Online 1 to 1

https://www.englishonline1to1.com

Book a *FREE* introductory session so we can discuss your needs!

Friendly, Personalised Lessons to Improve your English

Contents

<u>Preface</u>

The idioms and phrases are grouped by situations/contexts in which you might meet them:

Preface

Several years ago, while working in my first job as a teacher of English as a Foreign Language in Turkey, the headteacher, Mr Abdullah, used to delight in collaring me whenever it rained so that he could use his one phrase of English. You've guessed it!

"It's raining cats and dogs!".

He showed his delight at this crazy expression by guffawing loudly and repeating it to whichever teachers or pupils were within earshot. I didn't have the heart to tell him that it wasn't one I used or one I heard many people use these days.

Using idioms and colloquial phrases are so much part of the English language. We use them naturally, without thinking. In fact, I used one in the paragraph above! Mr Abdullah used to collar me'. I would probably think twice about using it now when working overseas. The longer I have worked abroad, the more I have come to hesitate before using an idiom or colloquial phrase with non-native English speaking friends and colleagues, even those whose English is pretty fluent. All too often, the expression goes right over their heads (there's another everyday expression which just came naturally– over their heads!)

I compiled the following collection of common English Idioms and Colloquialisms many years ago when I worked in Italy and was invited to do a seminar at a private language school for Italian State Teachers. The brief was to do a fun but useful session - and that is what it proved to be! I have since used the collection with teenage and adult students and non-native English teachers as a basis for creating role-play. The performances have frequently been hilarious!

The idioms and phrases are grouped by situations/contexts i which you might meet them, covering general conversation, expressing feelings and understanding, problems, solutions, relationships and time expressions. They should prove useful t non-native speakers in making sense of our rich and often funny English language. After all, learning English isn't exactly "a piece of cake"!

....

I have indicated whether the particular saying is an idiom or phrasal verb, although often phrasal verbs can be classed as idioms. The Cambridge English Dictionary Online gives the following definitions:

IDIOM: a group of words in a fixed order that has a particular meaning that is different from the meanings of each word on its own: For example, to "have bitten off more than you can chew" is an idiom that means you have tried to do something too difficult for you.

PHRASAL VERB: a phrase that consists of a verb with a preposition or adverb or both, the meaning of which is different from the meaning of its separate parts.

Of course, the collection is far from exhaustive, but hopefully, it will prove useful to non-native speakers in making sense of our complex, often funny, English language.

Unless you were brought a country where English is the main language, it's probably 'pie in the sky' to believe that you will ever master the many thousands. And even then, there are differences between English speaking countries. Although many are the same, there are lots of British and American idiomatic expressions which are native to each country. This collection is of British English expressions.

This book provides a start with some of the common ones sed the UK.

COMMON ENGLISH IDIOMS

AND

COLLOQUIALISMS

I = Idiom

PV = Phrasal Verb

Sometimes they can be both.

CONVERSATION

(It's) just not on I

Not an appropriate way of behaving

A piece of cake I

Extremely easy

Answer back PV

Reply rudely. Used in the negative with children to say, "Don't answer back!"

At a push I

Probably possible, but difficult

Can take it or leave it I

You don't hate something, but you don't particularly like it either

Cheer up! I

Said to someone who is looking miserable or feeling down to suggest that they be happier!

Child's play I

Extremely easy

Come off it! I

Said when you disagree or feel impatient with someone

Cut a long story short I

Tell the main points, but not all the details

Don't make me laugh! I

You think something is unlikely

Don't push your luck I

Don't try too hard to get what you want and risk losing what you have achieved (also used to tell someone not to 'push' you too far as you are getting annoyed, although it can also be used humorously in this way)

Fire away! PV

Start speaking!

Get a life I

Find more interesting things to do I

Get a move on I

Hurry up

Get on with you! I

Said (sometimes, but not always jokingly) when you disagree or feel impatient with someone

Getting at (what are you're getting at?) (I don't know what you're getting at) PV

Asking someone what they mean, usually because they have said something indirectly

Hang on! PV

Wait!

Hard (heavy) going I

Difficult, needs a lot of effort

Have a go/try/bash I

Try to do something

If all else fails I

If all other plans do not work

If I were in your shoes I

If I were in your position

If need be I

If it is really necessary

It's neither here nor there I

It's not very important

Just my luck I

Said (sometimes humorously) to mean you are always unlucky

Lighten up! PV
Said to encourage someone who is being over-serious or annoyed

Like I need a hole in my head (I need it like I need ...) I
don't need it at all and don't want it

Long time, no see! I
Haven't seen you for a long time

No such luck! I
Disappointed you were not able to do something

Not worth my (your) while I
Will not benefit from doing it

One way or the other, I'll … I
You're not sure how exactly but it will happen

Six of one and half a dozen of the other I
Two people or groups are equally responsible for a situation (just as bad as each other)

Steady on! PV
Said to someone if you think what you think they are saying is a bit extreme or to tell them to slow down.

That's life! I
Bad things happen and you can't prevent them.

You can say that again! I
You totally agree

You could've fooled me! I
You don't really believe

FEELINGS: HAPPINESS, SADNESS, ANGER, MIXED

Drive someone up the wall I

Make someone very angry

Fed up I

To be bored or angry because a bad situation has continued for too long or a subject has been discussed too much. It can also mean sad, down, depressed.

Feel down I/PV

Feel sad

Get you down PV

When something gets you down, it upsets you, makes you unhappy

Give someone a piece of your mind I

Tell someone how angry you are with them

Hard done by I/PV

If you feel hard done by, you feel that you have not been treated fairly, you feel sorry for yourself

Learnt my lesson I

Something bad has happened and you have decided never to let it happen again

Makes your day (something) I

If something makes your day, it makes you extremely happy

Mixed feelings I

Sometimes feel positive, sometimes not

Not the end of the world I

It won't cause serious problems

Over the moon I

Extremely happy/excited

Thrilled to bits |

Extremely happy/excited

KNOWING, UNDERSTANDING, PROBLEMS, SOLUTIONS

A fact of life |

An unpleasant situation that has to be accepted because it cannot be changed

Be that as it may |

Means you accept that something is true, but it still does not change your opinion

Be-all-and-end-all |

The most important thing (used NEGATIVELY ... not the be-all and-end-all)

Come a long way |

Made good progress

Come up against a brick wall |

Something is blocking you from what I want to do

Does the trick |

Solves a problem

Easier said than done |

Something you say when something seems like a good idea but is actually challenging to do

Faintest idea (don't have the) |

Don't really know at all

Fall into place |

You understand something you did not understand before or everything goes well

Figment of your imagination |

Something you have imagined which is not true

Get around (something) PV

Find a way of dealing with or avoiding a problem

Get hold of the wrong end of the stick (to) |

Come to the wrong conclusion

Get round to PV

Do something you need to or have intended to do for sometime

Get to grips with |

Make an effort to understand or deal with a situation or problem

Get your own way |

Persuade other people to let you do what you want

Go round in circles |

Making no progress in an argument or discussion

Got the message (has) |

Someone finally becomes aware of a fact (often used with unpleasant facts)

In a nutshell |

Describing as briefly as possible; succinctly

Knickers in a twist |

If you tell someone not to get their knickers in a twist (and can be to a man, as well as a woman!), you are telling them not to get extremely upset about something.

Learnt my lesson |

Something bad has happened and you decided never to let it happen again

Makes all the difference (to something) |

Has a very positive effect on a situation or a thing

Not a clue (about) |

Don't really know at all

On the one (other) hand |

Used to present two opposite facts or two different ways of looking at the same issue

Out of your depth |

In a situation or facing a problem that is too complicated/difficult to deal with

Put my foot in it I

Said something tactless and embarrassing

Put two and two together I

Come to a conclusion from known facts

Second thoughts (to have) I

Decided something but no longer sure about; to change one's mind

Sink in PV

If something starts to sink in you are starting to understand it (is it sinking in?)

Take in/take something (it) in PV

Look at something carefully, noticing all the details. Understand something (having considered it carefully)

Teach him/her a lesson I

Someone does something stupid which affects them in a way that they'll never want to do it again

RELATIONSHIPS

At cross-purposes (Talk/be) I

Not understanding each other because trying to do or say different things

Be in someone's good books I

The person is pleased with you – possibly only temporarily

Break off with PV

End a relationship

Call round PV

Visit someone who lives nearby

Drop round/drop in PV

Make a short visit to someone in their home often without arranging it beforehand

Fall out (with) PV

Have a disagreement with (can also be used as a noun, e.g. They have had a fall-out.

Finish with (someone) PV

End a relationship

Get at (someone) PV

Criticise

Get on with PV

To have a good relationship with

Get together with PV

To meet to do something

Hang out with PV

Spend time with

Hard time (give someone a) I

Make things unpleasant for someone

Have a soft spot for I

Feel a lot of affection for someone

Keep oneself to oneself I

Prefer to be on one's own and avoid talking with or doing thing with other people. Private.

Let (someone) down PV

Disappoint by not acting or behaving as they want or expect you to do

Make up (with) PV

Forgive and become friends again

Rub someone up the wrong way I

Irritate someone

To get on like a house on fire with someone I/PV

To have an excellent relationship with

Wind (someone) up PV

Tell someone something (often that is not true) to annoy or tease them

TIME

(For) once and for all |
Finally and definitely

At the end of the day |
Something you say before stating an important fact or idea

Call it a day |
Decide to finish

Don't have a minute to call your own |
Very busy indeed

For the time being |
Temporarily, instead of

Hold up PV
Delay

In the long run |
A long time from now; finally; eventually

It's early days, yet |
It's too soon to tell

Nine times out of ten |
Almost always

On and off/off and on |
Sometimes, but not regularly

Only a matter of time |
It will definitely happen, even though we can't say exactly when

Take time off PV

Spend time away from work

MISCELLANEOUS

A matter of opinion I

Something different people will have different opinions about (usually means you don't agree with the idea or statement)

A rip off I

Not worth what you paid for it. Can mean probably cheated

Believe my eyes (can't) (couldn't) I
Couldn't believe what I was seeing

Bet (I) I

Used to indicate that you are pretty sure that something is true happened or will happen

Call back (on the telephone) PV

To call/telephone again

Chat up PV

Talk in a way to someone that shows you are (sexually) attracted to them to try to make them attracted to you too. Flirt with someone.

Cost a small fortune I

Very expensive

Cost an arm and a leg I

Very expensive

Deals with PV

If something (a book, article, film) deals with a particular subject, it is about that subject. Negative meaning: to deal with someone is to confront him or her, to chastise

Get a word in edgeways (can't) I

Difficult to tell something to someone because they continue talking when you try to speak

Get away with PV

Succeed in not being criticised, found out or punished for something wrong that you have done

Get behind PV

Get behind with work means not done as much as you should have

Get by PV

Manage on little money, or generally manage despite difficulties

Get out of PV

Avoid doing something you should do, often by giving an excuse

Get through (on the telephone) PV

To make a connection

Go along with someone/something   PV

Support and idea, agree

Gone from bad to worse I

Got even worse than it was before

Hold your horses! I

Wait! Don't be impatient!

In the same boat (be) I

Be in the same, usually difficult situation

Jog someone's memory I

Make them remember something

Jot down PV

Make notes (so you'll remember it)

Look up PV

Search for (as in lookup/search for a word in a dictionary

Make something up PV

Invent, tell a lie

Make the best of a bad job I

Be positive about a situation that you do not like but cannot change

Make up your mind I

Decide

Mess about PV

Spend time doing things with no particular purpose. Often used negatively. Students may be messing about when they are behaving stupidly or wasting time doing unimportant things.

Miles away I

Not concentrating, thinking about something else

Mind goes blank I

Can't think of anything to say

Miss the point (to) I

Misunderstand the main thing

Off the top of my head I

Without thinking deeply, a quick response

On the face of it I

Superficially; according to the appearance of something

On the same wavelength I

Think alike

On the tip of your tongue I

You know it but can't quite remember it

Phone up PV

Make a call

Plain sailing (be) I

Be very easy

play it by ear I

respond to the situation as it occurs, without planning; don't decide what to do beforehand

pop in PV

go into a place for a short time

put (someone) off PV

Make someone not like something

put (something or someone) off PV

postpone

put up with PV

accept unpleasant behaviour or an unpleasant situation even though you do not like it

ring off (on the telephone) PV

end a call

rushed off my feet I

very busy

screw up PV

Make a mess of a task; fail

second best   I

Not as good as the thing you really want

shows off PV

Tries to make people admire his/her abilities or achievements in a way other people find annoying. Also, a noun, a 'show-off' is someone who tries to impress

slip your mind I

Forget about something

snowed under I

very busy

take up/take something up PV

Start something (new)

Talk (something) over PV *Discuss*

Text back PV

Send a text (SMS) message in reply (British people called SM messages Texts)

To be on about I/PV

To talk about something (often used negatively as in "I didn't know what he was on about" i.e. what he was talking about.

To take the Mickey (out of someone) I

To make fun of, to tease, mock

Turn down PV

Refuse an offer

Up to my eyes in (work) (it) I

Very busy

Work cut out (to have your) I

Have something very difficult to do, achieve

Worst comes to the worst (if the) I

If the situation becomes serious

or friendly, personalised, one -to- one video lessons to help you improve your English
Please visit:

English Online 1 to 1

https://www.englishonline1to1.com

Book a *FREE* introductory session so we can discuss your needs!

ENGLISH ONLINE 1 TO 1

Friendly, Personalised Lessons to Improve your English

Thanks,

Steve Ellis

Printed in Dunstable, United Kingdom

73140316R00020